U.K. DV

HIGHWAY

DRIVERS TEST QUESTIONS

AND ANSWERS

A guide on how to pass your driving test with Over 220 drivers test theory questions and answers extracted from DVSA manual.

By

Theodore. G. Armstrong

Copyright

Table of Contents

Introduction

Understanding the functions of part of a vehicle is, key to begins your driving experience. Therefore having adequate knowledge of how to drive on the road is necessary to avoid any form of accident.

Every driver is required to have adequate information and theoretical knowledge of driving before proceeding to the road for the real driving experience.

This book provides selected test question for potential drivers to study and be ready to succeed in the theory part of the driving test. With the theoretical knowledge, the practical part of the test would be easy to handle.

Go through the material more than once for proper absorption of the content therein.

Enjoy your ride.

Chapter 1

Alertness

1) **If your phone rings while driving, you should?**

    a) Come to a complete stop

    b) Pick the phone with your left hand and answer.

    c) Look for a suitable place and pull up

    d) Pull up at the nearest fuel station

2) **What is the work of the yellow lines painted across the road, and you can see these lines close to a roundabout or a dangerous junction?**

    a) It helps you choose the correct lane.

    b) It helps you keep the correct separation distance.

    c) It makes you adjust your speed.

    d) It tells you the distance to the roundabout.

3) **Why do you give enough space when following a large vehicle?**

    a) To allow the driver of the large vehicle to see you.

    b) To see the road ahead clearly.

c) To pass either side of the large vehicle.

d) All of the above

4) **It is important to check your mirrors regularly. Why?**

   a) To stop abruptly

   b) To have a clue on what can happen next.

   c) To check your passengers.

   d) To accelerate faster when overtaken.

5) **When approaching a T-Junction, you noticed that cars parked along the road, make it difficult for you to view the oncoming vehicle. How best will you enter your proposed lane?**

   a) Slowly drive forward and keep looking until there is a gap to enter your proposed lane.

   b) Slowly drive across to your proposed lane while the oncoming vehicle slows down for you.

   c) Allow a pedestrian to direct you when there is space for you to drive in.

   d) Sound your horn as you drive across to your proposed lane.

6) **A traffic light has been on green for some time. What should you do as you approach the traffic light?**

a) Ignore the traffic light

b) Maintain your speed

c) Prepare to stop

d) Accelerate more

7) **Which of the following do you consider before pulling up on the road?**

a) Check the mirror

b) Give the correct signal.

c) Assess what is ahead

d) All of the above

8) **You should avoid pasting stickers on the driver's side of the windscreen because:**

a) They cause a distraction for the driver.

b) They enable the police to have access to them.

c) They add extra protection against sunlight.

d) They reduce your field of vision.

9) **A lapse of concentration while driving can cause by one of the following?**

a) Sleep driving

b) Talking passenger

c) Oncoming vehicle

d) Car radio

10) While on a long journey, there is a high possibility of feeling sleepy at the steering wheel. How best could you avoid sleeping off while driving

   a) Ensure the air conditioning is on

   b) Find a place to rest along the journey.

   c) Keep busy with chewing gum.

   d) Have passengers that will keep you busy

11) You are approaching a junction and observe that there is a vehicle moving slower than yours. What should you do?

   a) Overtake the vehicle quickly

   b) Follow the vehicle until after the junction.

   c) Sound your horn to alert the driver

   d) Drive closer to the front vehicle to make it move faster

12) Which of the conditions below should be avoided? Overtaken....

   a) After a bend

   b) In a one-way street

   c) On a 30-mph road

   d) When approaching a ditch

13) You are driving for a family visit, and suddenly your phone ring. What should you do?

a) receive the call because it could be an emergency

b) Use your hand free kit and receive the call.

c) Slow down your speed and receive your call.

d) Park in a suitable place and receive your call.

14) **You are driving on a motorway, and your rear tyre suddenly burst. What must you do?**

a) Inform other road users by given a hand signal

b) Put the gear to neutral.

c) Take control of the vehicle and pull up by the shoulder.

d) Apply the brake while pulling up by the shoulder of the road.

15) **The rain is weighty, thus reducing your visibility. Which of the following action should you take as a defensive measure?**

a) Sound your horn intermittently.

b) Turn on your headlight.

c) Turn on your inner light.

d) Turn on your wiper

16) One of the following practices can cause distraction when driving?

    a)   Using a mobile phone

    b)   Listening to the radio

    c)   Speaking with passengers

    d)   Checking the mirror

17) When one of your passengers just had a seizure and needed urgent medical assistance. What should you do?

    a)   Call an emergency medical line.

    b)   Give the victim urgent medication.

    c)   Keep talking to the victim.

    d)   Park and ask for an assistant from a passerby.

18) What must you do before you make a U-turn?

    a)   Give both an arm signal and make use of your indicators.

    b)   always signal so that other drivers can slow down for you

    c)   always look over your shoulder for a final check

    d)   Select a higher gear than normal

19) While driving on a dual carriage road, you notice that the vehicle in front of you is moving slowly; thus, you need to change. What must you do before moving into a new lane?

    a)   Honk your horn to alert the car behind

    b)   Indicate the correct signal, slow down

    c)   Make use of your mirrors, look over your shoulder and indicate

    d)   Indicate, use all mirrors, look over your shoulder

20) What must you do as you drive past a cyclist on a narrow road?

    a)   Drive fast past the cyclist

    b)   Sound your horn and drive quickly pass the driver

    c)   Sound your horn as you passes, leaving enough room, and drive pass quickly.

    d)   Sound your horn as you passes, leaving enough room, and drive pass slowly.

21) Drivers are advised to look over their shoulder while driving. Why?

    a)   To check vehicles coming from behind.

    b)   To make up for blind spots.

    c)   To check on the mirror.

    d)   To alert the oncoming vehicle.

22) You must avoid distractions while driving at all times because:

    a) Road hazards can occur at any time.

    b) Hands-free phones can cause a lack of concentration.

    c) Lack of concentration improves your driving.

    d) Concentration diverts attention

23) You are trying to pull out into a major road at a T-Junction, but the windscreen pillar is restricts your view vision. To prevent an accident, which of the following road users should your pay attention to?

    a) Motorcyclist

    b) Pedestrian

    c) Cyclist

    d) All of the above

24) If you find yourself lost on an unfamiliar road, what action should you take?

    a) Bring out your map and check

    b) Turn on your Google map for direction.

c) Park safely and check a map

d) Ask a pedestrian at a traffic light.

25) **The design of the car can make it difficult to see clearly, especially at bends and junctions. What part of the car is known to cause such obstruction?**

a) The windscreen

b) The back mirror

c) The windscreen pillars

d) The bonnet

26) **If you find it difficult, getting an excellent all-around vision while turning, what should you do?**

a) Ask someone to guide you.

b) Use the reverse and side mirrors.

c) Open the door and view as you turn.

d) None of the above

27) **Before emerging right onto a dual carriageway, what must you be cautious of as you pull out?**

a) Make sure that the central reserve is wide enough.

b) Ensure your vehicle is visible to an oncoming vehicle

c) There are few vehicles on your path.

d) Make sure the vehicle behind has enough room.

28) To avoid drowsiness on the road while embarking on a long journey the following day, you must?

a) Prepare for a caffeinated drink to be taken as you journey.

b) Have enough night sleep and prepare for a place to rest

c) Plan to drive slowly and carefully to avoid an accident

d) All of the above

Answer To Questions on Alertness

No	1	2	3	4	5	6	7	8	9
Answer	C	C	D	B	A	C	D	D	A

No	10	11	12	13	14	15	16	17	18
Answer	B	B	D	D	C	B	A	A	B

No	19	20	21	22	23	24	25	26	27
Answer	D	D	B	A	D	C	C	A	A

No	28
Answer	B

Chapter 2

Attitude

1) Pelican crossings are a type of signal-controlled crossings operated by pedestrians. They have no red-amber stage before green. But instead, they have flashing amber lights. What must you do when you get to the crossing and meet flashing amber light but, the crossing is clear?

    a) Continue driving ahead.

    b) Wait for the green light to show.

    c) Wait for a pedestrian to cross before continuing.

    d) Stop for the red light is about to show.

2) When you drive up to a pedestrian crossing, you should:

    a) Slow down and prepare to stop

    b) Drive on not to obstruct vehicles coming behind yours

    c) Sound your horn to alert the pedestrian that you are crossing

    d) Stop and wave the pedestrian to cross the road.

3) Why should you not wave on the pedestrian to cross the road when you stop at a pedestrian crossing?

a) Another vehicle moving along the road may not have seen them.

b) Another vehicle moving along the road may not have seen your signal to the pedestrian.

c) Another vehicle moving along the road may not be able to stop safely.

d) All of the above

4) 'Tailgating' is considered an unsafe practice in driving. Why?

a) It causes speeding, which can cause road accident.

b) It leaves the tailboard or boot of a car open, which can lead to an accident.

c) It makes vehicles to follow a lead vehicle too close, which can cause an accident.

d) It leaves the hazard light unnecessarily, which can confuse other road users leading to an accident.

5) Following a box body truck too close is considered a dangerous practice because:

a) You will be forced to move at its speed.

b) It will restrict your view of the road ahead.

c) It leads to boredom as the box body trucks are slow-moving.

d) It can lead to an engine problem.

6) It started raining heavily two minutes ago, and my car is following another car at a steady speed of 60mph. What time gap should I give to the vehicle in front to minimize the risk of hitting on it from behind?

a) One second

b) Two seconds

c) Three seconds

d) Four seconds

7) On a dry and bright Saturday afternoon on your way to a beach, which is 60km from your home and along a highway? What is the time gap you should give between your car and the car in front of you for safety?

a) One second

b) Two seconds

c) Three seconds

d) Four seconds

8) When a long, heavy laden vehicle is taken time to overtake you, you should:

a) Slow down for the vehicle to overtake.

b) Maintain the same speed.

c) Allow it takes its time to overtake.

d) Change direction to stop him.

9) What should you do when an ambulance flashing blue beacon is following your vehicles?

a) Stop immediately for the vehicle to pass.

b) Pullover if it is safe to do so.

c) Maintain your speed until the vehicle find a way for itself to overtake.

d) Avoid being overtaken by accelerating harder.

10) Which vehicle is more at risk on a road where the tram operates?

a) Cycles

b) Lorries

c) Buses

d) Cars

11) You are not advised to use your horn in one of the following situations.

a) When there is danger before you.

b) When you are parked but obstructed.

c) When you need to indicate your presence.

d) All of the above

12) You are on a one-way street, and you wish to turn to your right. Which position of lane should you take after turning?

a) Centralize your vehicle along the road

b) In the left- hand lane

c) In the right-hand lane

d) Any position along the road

13) Moving to a correct position on time before turning is the right thing to do for the following reason?

   a) It helps other road users to know your intention to take the necessary action.

   b) To enable other road users to give you the chance to turn.

   c) To enable you to have a better view of the road ahead of you.

   d) It helps secure a safe turning radius for your vehicle.

14) What is a toucan crossing?

   a) It is the same as the Zebra crossing.

   b) It is a crossing for vehicles and cyclists.

   c) It is a crossing for cyclists.

   d) It is a crossing for pedestrians and cyclists.

15) The legal speed limit along a road is posted on the road. You were driving within the legal speed limit when you observed a vehicle flashing its headlight behind you. You should:

   a) Allow the vehicle to pass.

   b) Speed up to create enough room behind you

   c) Pullover and stop for the vehicle to pass.

   d) Maintain your speed

16) Which of the following indicates the correct use of the headlight?

a) Greeting other road users.

b) Show others of their actions on the road.

c) Give priority to other road users.

d) To alert others of your presence.

17) What should you do when you arrived at a junction and observed that hedges and walls had obstructed your view?

a) Maintain your normal speed but stay in the middle of the road

b) Slow down and keep to the right.

c) Slow down and look to your right.

d) Slow down, then observe both sides of the road.

18) The two-second rule is:

a) The time gap between the vehicle ahead of you and your vehicle.

b) The time needed to join the road at a junction after stopping.

c) The time needed to join an adjacent road after stopping.

d) All of the above

19) You arrived at a puffin crossing, and the light turn's red: the next light that will follow is:

a) The amber light

b) The flashing red light

c) The green light

d) The yellow light

20) When travelling on a clear night with no sign of vehicle light from oncoming traffic ahead of you, which light should you use?

a) Fog light

b) Hazard light

c) Full beam headlight

d) All of the above

21) What should you do when you want to turn to a street on the left, and immediately a long vehicle steered to the right?

a) Pass the vehicle using the available space created on the left.

b) Sound your horn to alert the long vehicle driver that you are passing.

c) Maintain your speed while sounding your horn and your headlight turned on.

d) Slow down while you allow the long vehicle to turn.

22) You observed that a vehicle is coming too close behind you. What should you?

a) Maintain the same speed or slow down

b) Speed up to avoid being hit from behind

c) Move to the other lane

d) Wave the drive to slow down

23) Why is it not advisable to park or drive in a bus lane even when a bus is not at sight?

a) To avoid disruption of traffic.

b) To avoid delay in public transport.

c) All of the above

d) None of the above

24) When you come across a herder with his animal, and he beckons on you to slow down. What should you do?

a) Slow down and pass when it is safe

b) Ignore the herder

c) Pass as quickly as possible

d) Stop until the herder asks you to go.

25) You are drive along a less busy road; you came across a horse with its rider moving parallel along your lane but closer to the external road marking. What should you do?

a) Maintain your lane

b) Sound your horn to alert the rider and the horse of your presence

c) Safely pass the horse, giving enough room from the horse.

d) Inform the rider of his closeness to the road

26) You arrived at a Zebra crossing and observed that Pedestrians are waiting to cross. You should:

a) Stop and beckon on them to cross.

b) Flag down other vehicles to stop at the crossing.

c) Flash your headlight for them to cross.

d) Slow down and ready to stop

27) On which of the following conditions will you give the 2 seconds gap between the vehicle in front and your vehicle?

a) Wet condition

b) Dry condition

c) Damp condition

d) Humid condition

28) What is defensive driving?

a) Defending your position and lane while driving to avoid other vehicles from reckless entry

b) Using your hazard light and horn to alert other road users of your presence

c) By questioning the actions of other road users and being prepared for the unexpected

d) Being ready to call the authority on the recklessness of other vehicles that could endanger the life of others

29) Which of the following is the most difficult aspect of driving?

a) Competitive

b) Responsible

c) Considerate

d) Defensive

30) **The rain has just stopped, and there is an effect of glare on the wet road. What would you do if the glare affects you?**

a) Move quickly past the areas where the glare is affecting your vision.

b) Use your wiper to clean the windshield.

c) Slow down or pull over if necessary.

d) Use your hazard to alert other road users of the danger on the road.

31) **You are going to work on a Monday morning; a car suddenly overtakes you and pulls back into the traffic in front of you. What should you do?**

a) Overtake the car in front quickly to avoid hitting it from behind.

b) Hoot for about three seconds to alert the driver of reckless driving.

c) Slow down and increase the gap between your car the one in front.

d) Show your frustration by flashing your headlight and hooting for two seconds.

32) **A driver approaches a two-lane roundabout and needs to turn on the first exit on the left but, in front of him is a long vehicle signaling left but occupies both lanes of the road. What will be the driver's position?**

a) The driver should position in the right lane following the signal of the long vehicle.

b) The driver should position on the right lane, signaling right.

c) The driver should position on the left lane while waiting for the long vehicle to complete its turn.

d) The driver should position on the left lane while signaling to the left.

33) **A driver driving a long vehicle turns left at a roundabout and occupies both lanes of the road on the process. While should the driver take such action?**

a) The steering of the vehicle is probably stiff and difficult to turn.

b) The driver does not want to be overtaken.

c) The driver was probably confused on the road to take

d) The driver was trying to achieve the turning radius of the vehicle.

34) **While driving along a busy road, you saw people crossing the road at a point where there is no zebra crossing, and it's illegal to cross at that point. What should you do?**

a) Slow down and stop for the pedestrians to finish crossing

b) Maintain the same speed and let the pedestrian take the necessary action

c) Speed up to scare the pedestrians

d) Sound your horn and flash your headlight to alert the pedestrians of reckless crossing

Answers To Questions on Atitude

No	1	2	3	4	5	6	7	8	9
Answers	A	A	D	C	B	D	B	A	B

No	10	11	12	13	14	15	16	17	18
Answers	A	B	C	A	D	A	D	D	A

No	19	20	21	22	23	24	25	26	27
Answers	C	C	D	A	C	A	C	D	B

No	28	29	30	31	32	33	34
Answers	D	A	C	C	D	D	A

Chapter 3

Safety and your vehicle

1) What time at night is it illegal to sound your horn unless it is necessary to do so?

    a) Between 10.30 pm to 6.30 am

    b) Between 11.30 pm to 7.30 am

    c) Between 10.30 pm to 7.00 am

    d) Between 11.30 pm to 7.00 am

2) One of the following is an environmentally friendly means of transportation.

    a) Bus

    b) Tram

    c) Train

    d) Motorbike

3) Road accidents become fatal when a vehicle is traveling at a higher speed than at a low speed. Which of the following is a control measure to reduce the speed of vehicles on the road?

    a) Zebra crossing

    b) Traffic lights

    c) Road humps

    d) Road narrowing

4) When are you advised to use a parking light at night while driving?

a) When the allowable speed limit less than 20 mph.

b) When the allowable speed limit is less than 30 mph.

c) When the allowable speed limit is more than 30 mph.

d) When the allowable speed limit is less than 10mph.

5) **You are advised to park in the direction of traffic flow to enable other road users to see the reflectors on your vehicle's rear. How true is this advice?**

a) Very true

b) Not very true

c) False

d) Indifference

6) **When topping up your battery liquid level, you should:**

a) Top up with cool water

b) Top up with acid water

c) Top up with distill water

d) Top up with alkaline water

7) **What level should you top up the water level in your battery?**

a) Just before the cell plate

b) Half to the top of the cell plate

c) Up to the top of the battery

d) Above the cell plate

8) **Are catalytic converters designed for one of the following purposes?**
   a) Clean up the engine
   b) Reduce fuel consumption
   c) Reduce toxic emission
   d) Improve engine wear

9) **Checking the tyre pressure is important for safety reasons. When is the right time to check the pressure of your tyres?**
   a) After a long journey
   b) When the tyres are hot
   c) When the tyres are cold
   d) When the tyres have been suspended

10) **One of the following can add to an increase in fuel consumption?**
    a) Overinflated tyres
    b) Under-inflated tyres
    c) Newly mounted tyres
    d) All of the above

11) **You can reduce fuel consumption by applying one of the following actions.**
    a) Accelerating and braking gently and smoothly.
    b) Quick acceleration and breaking.
    c) Maintaining a high speed.

d) High vehicle rev.

12) You can achieve a 15% reduction in fuel consumption by practicing one of the following.

a) Using your horn only when necessary.

b) Obeying traffic sign and regulation.

c) Checking on your vehicles regularly.

d) Using your controls smoothly.

13) Pleasant journey, comfortable journey, and journey with less congestion are the benefit of the following?

a) Listening to the weather forecast

b) Journey planning beforehand

c) Reading vehicle manual

d) Liaising with other drivers

14) While driving, you should be anticipating a change in advance to …..?

a) Reduce fuel consumption

b) Avoid rapid acceleration and braking.

c) Increase pollution

d) Avoid pedestrian crossing.

15) Fluids are of utmost importance in vehicles for various reasons. It is advisable to check your fluid level regularly. Which of the following fluid depletion can lead to potential road crash?

a) Radiator

b) Anti-freeze

c) Brake

d) Fuel

16) **When the brake fluid reservoir is a drop below the minimum level, what will be its effect on the car?**

a) Air could enter the hydraulic system.

b) The remaining fluid in the reservoir could start foaming.

c) The car begins to jerk

d) The brake system begins to overheat.

17) **Uneven wear on tyres can be as a result of one of the following.**

a) Bad suspension

b) passengers

c) Bad brake system

d) Wheel alignment

18) **To avoid the braking system's loss of efficiency while driving on a steep and downhill stretch of**

road, which of the following gear should you use?

a) High gear

b) Low gear

c) Neutral

d) Reverser gear

19) If your car is fitted with the brake drum, which of the following could make the drum get hot, thus leading to the brake losing traction on the wheel?

a) Lack of service

b) Inefficient gear

c) Long hours of use

d) Faded tyres

20) When this sign shows in your dashboard, it represents:

a) Warning

b) The engine might be having a problem

c) The lighting systems should be checked

d) Possible fault in the braking system

21) You observed that your vehicle always bounce when you turn at a roundabout.

When you press down the front wing further, the bouncing continues. What could be the problem?

    a)   Worn out suspension

    b)   Uneven tyres

    c)   Poorly aligned tyres

    d)   Overloaded vehicle

22) **How would you dispose of the old engine oil after servicing your car.?**

    a)   Dispose of in the drainage

    b)   Dip hole and pour it in

    c)   Discharge it in the septic system

    d)   Take it to a local-authority site

23) **Tyres are manufactured with tread to give a good grip on the road surface. What is the minimum legal depth of the grip on the tyres?**

    a)   1.00 mm

    b)   1.60 mm

    c)   2.00 mm

    d)   2.60 mm

24) **Which one of the following is the benefit of wearing suitable and comfortable shoes while driving?**

   a) Adjust the seat to the right position

   b) To enable you to seek help should a fault occurs in a wrong location

   c) Make you have control of the vehicle foot pedals

   d) Suitable shoes should be based on the weather situation at the time

25) **What is the function of a head restraint in a car seat?**

   a) To enable the driver to hang jackets and pullovers

   b) Reduce the risk of head injury during a collision

   c) Enable the driver to adjust the head restraint for driving comfort

   d) To protect the back passenger during a collision

26) **If you are carrying an adult and a 13-years old child in a vehicle, who should be held responsible for the child not being on a seat belt?**

   a) The driver

   b) The adult

   c) The 13-years old

   d) The driver and the adult

27) The environment needs combined effort to be safe for all. As a driver, which of the following are you supposed to do to protect the environment?

a) By accelerating gently.

b) Regular servicing of a vehicle.

c) Reducing driving speed

d) All of the above

28) Fuel costs money, and wasting it ignorantly in common. One of the following actions can cause wastage of fuel?

a) Well inflated tyres

b) Reduce the weight on the vehicle

c) Roof rack

d) Braking and accelerating smoothly

29) The anti-lock system is less effective on the wheel in one of the following surfaces.

a) Slippery surface

b) Loose surface

c) Wet surface

d) Dry surface

30) What should you do if you observe that your vehicle pulls to one side when you apply brake?

a) Use the hand brake

b) Pump the brake pedal

c) Take the car for a check

d) Exchange the front and rear tyres

31) You are driving at a certain speed. You observed that your car steering is vibrating. It is a sign of which of the following faults?

a) Wheel balancing

b) Worn shock absorber

c) Bad brake system

d) Weak clutch system

32) You planned to spend about five minutes at a grocery store. You drove to the store, stepped out of your car, locked it, and took a second look inside the car; found out that you have your laptop on the front seat. What should you do next?

a) Inform the police

b) Reposition the laptop where it could not be seen from outside

c) Quickly go in and buy what you need

d) Make sure all the doors are locked to prevent someone from breaking in

33) To discourage car thieves from stealing your car, which of the following practice will deter the thieves from stealing your car?

a) Provide tinted glasses on all the door windows

b) Make sure the inner light is on all the time

c) Always have the security emblem on your windscreen

d) Etch your car registration numbers on all your windscreen

34) You should always leave the following in the car except:

a) Vehicle documents

b) First aid kit

c) Route map

d) Tax disc

35) You should always park your car in one of the following places?

a) filling station

b) police station

c) secured car park

d) At a busy place

36) What is dry steering?

a) Driving on a dry road

b) A sign of lack of steering oil

c) Turning your vehicle at a very sharp curve

d) Turning the steering of a stationary vehicle

37) A vehicle engine rate of pollution increases when it has not reached its normal running temperature. While going on a short distance, you should do the following to avoid pollution of the environment?

a) Using a motor bike

b) Driving slowly

c) Accelerating and braking smoothly

d) Take a walk or use a bike

38) Car thieves get easily attracted to car radio. Which of the following approach is best to deter car thieves from stealing your car radio?

a) Park your car in a garage

b) Always lock your car when it is parked

c) Use a security coded radio

d) None of the above

39) **Because you care about the environment and keen to reduce the emission of toxic gas while driving, which of the following mean will be of greater help to you in achieving your aim?**

a) Using a scientifically approved oil filter

b) Using a catalytic converter

c) Braking and accelerating smoothly

d) Using a motor bike

40) Oil is mandatory for car engine to function effectively. What will be the effect of too much oil in the engine?

a) It will cause too much pressure in the engine thereby protecting the engine seal

b) It will cause too low pressure in the engine thereby affecting oil cover

c) It will cause too low pressure in the engine thereby cause oil leak

d) It will cause too much pressure in the engine thereby cause oil leak

41) **Ecosafe driving is:**
   a) Driving with no fuel
   b) Becoming more environmentally friendly driver
   c) Becoming more environmentally helpful by parking under a tree
   d) By driving to arrive at your destination faster to avoid causing traffic congestion

42) **You need to pick a parcel at a shop along the road. This will take you approximately 30 seconds. What should you do after parking in front of the shop?**
   a) Leave the steaming to allow the engine attain its running temperature
   b) Park the car but leave the two front window a bit lower to allow for the circulation of air
   c) Leave the car headlight and hazard light on after parking
   d) Switch off the engine, remove the key then lock the door

43) **Before you park at a parking lot, what should you do?**

a) Make sure your vehicle manual allows you to park at the parking lot

b) Make sure the hazard light is turned on

c) Make sure there is no restriction marking

d) Make sure that you are directed to park by a qualified traffic controller

44) **What is the work of a properly adjusted head restraint of a vehicle?**

a) It provides the driver with a good head rest

b) It stops the driver from following asleep

c) It provides comfort for the driver

d) It avoids neck injury during accident

45) **To reduce the possibility of your vehicle being broken into, which of the following is the best initial approach?**

a) Leave the engine running to deter car thieves

b) Take all valuables along with you

c) Move all valuable to the back seat

d) Leave all valuables on the floor

46) **Airbags are a must have for every vehicles to reduce sudden impact during collision. One of the following situations does not require an airbag.**

a) When a disable passenger is in the vehicle

b) When the engine becomes too hot

c) Where a baby seat is positioned

d) When passengers are less

47) **You will gain one of the following by looking well ahead of you while driving.**

a) You are more aware of hazards and plan ahead.

b) You determine how to overtake the vehicle ahead of you.

c) It enables the avoidance of spill on the motorway.

d) It is useful when short sightedness is involve.

48) **A properly serviced and maintained vehicle helps the environment to**

a) Avoid accidental tyre burst

b) Reduce glare while driving

c) Reduce toxic emission

d) Reduce water wastage

49) **You want to embark on a long journey, which of the following must be checked?**

a) Fuel, water level, seat alignment, oil

b) Oil, water level, air conditioner, tyre

c) Tyre, fuel, oil, water level

d) Tyre, oil, water, seat alignment

50) **Getting a place to park in a busy town is always tough. Suddenly you find a place with the zigzag line before a zebra crossing. Is it lawful to park at the space within the zigzag line?**

a) It is unlawful to park there

b) It safe because other vehicles could still go

c) The zigzag line allows you to park before the pedestrian

d) You are not to park on the zebra crossing to avoid interfering with the pedestrians

51) Rush hour is hectic part of the day. What is the effect of travelling outside the rush hour?

a) It shortens your time of travel.

b) It increases your time of travel.

c) It reduces toxic emission.

d) It reduces acceleration and braking time.

52) A type of line on a Red Route that prohibits stopping to park, load/unload, or board and alight from a vehicle at any time?

a) Yellow line

b) Double yellow lines

c) Redline

d) Double red line

53) You can stop to park, load/unload, or board and alight from a vehicle at the approved time indicated on the board on a Red Route. Such locations are marked by which type of line.

a) Single red line

b) Broken single red line

c) Broken double red line

d) Zigzag red line

54) Some routes have been designated special names. What is the name given to major roads to reduce obstruction of traffic flow, congestion, and inconsistent parking?

a) Yellow route

b) Double yellow route

c) Red route

d) Double red route

55) What should you do when you come across a junction with non- functioning traffic lights?

a) Drive as fast as possible to avoid an accident.

b) Drive with care before crossing

c) Wait for the traffic light to be switched on

d) Maintain your right of way

56) What is the effect of under-inflated tyres on your vehicle

a) Smooth ride

b) Seemingly heavy steering

c) Brake failure

d) Leak of the brake oil

57) What is the possible consequence of leaving a valuable to the eye of a passerby?

a) It will be admired

b) It attracts the attention of people

c) Your car could be broken into

d) Make sure the doors are locked

58) **One of the following should be deployed to avoid a direct collision with steering wheel, dashboard or door.**

a)   Seat cushion

b)   Steering wheel

c)   Airbag

d)   None of the above

Answers To Questions on Safety and your Vehicle

No	1	2	3	4	5	6	7	8	9
Answers	D	B	C	C	A	C	D	C	C

No	10	11	12	13	14	15	16	17	18
Answers	B	A	D	B	B	C	A	D	B

No	19	20	21	22	23	24	25	26	27
Answers	C	D	A	D	B	C	B	A	D

No	28	29	30	31	32	33	34	35	36
Answers	C	B	C	A	B	D	A	C	D

No	37	38	39	40	41	42	43	44	45
Answers	D	C	B	D	B	D	C	D	B

No	46	47	48	49	50	51	52	53	54
Answers	C	A	C	C	A	A	D	A	C

No	55	56	57	58
Answers	B	B	C	C

Chapter 4

Safety Margins

1) **What does the term 'coast' mean?**

   a) Driving along the seaside

   b) Driving with more attention to your environment and other road users

   c) Driving in a neutral or with the clutch disengaged

   d) Driving on a very high gear with a malfunctioning brake system

2) **What is the stopping distance of a vehicle?**

   a) Viewing time to braking time

   b) Driving speed and braking time

   c) Thinking time and braking time

   d) The time it takes to stop

3) **What should be your overall stopping distance when travelling on a good car at a speed of 70 mph on a good dry road surface?**

   a) 36 metres (118 feet)

   b) 53 metres (175 feet)

   c) 73 metres (240 feet)

   d) 96 metres (315 feet)

4) **What should be your overall stopping distance while driving at 60 mph on a sunny afternoon?**

   a) 36 metres (118 feet)

b) 53 metres (175 feet)

c) 73 metres (240 feet)

d) 96 metres (315 feet)

5) **What is the stopping distance for a car driving at 50 mph in good weather?**

a)   36 metres (118 feet)

b) 53 metres (175 feet)

c) 73 metres (240 feet)

d) 96 metres (315 feet)

6) **What is the stopping distance of a vehicle travelling at 30 mph?**

a) 12 metres (40 feet)

b) 23 metres (75 feet)

c) 36 metres (118 feet)

d) 53 metres (175 feet)

7) **In winter, the road becomes icy, and stopping distance is affected. Which of the following stopping distance is expected from the normal stopping distance?**

a) Three times

b) Five times

c) Eight times

d) Ten times

8) **Stopping distance increases on a wet road. For this reason, you created an ample gap to allow you to stop to avoid collision with the vehicle in**

front. If you observe that another vehicle pulls into the gap you have created, which of the following action is expected from you?

a) Close the gap before the vehicle pulls into the gap.

b) Overtake the vehicle as soon it pulls into your space.

c) Follow up with the speed of the over-taking vehicle.

d) Ease back for you to regain the expected gap.

9) In which of the following road are you likely to be affected by a strong gust of wind?

a) Hectic road

b) Forest road

c) Narrow road

d) Open stretch road?

10) One of the following road users will be most affected by the wind?

a) Cyclist

b) Motorist

c) Train

d) Tram

11) It is advisable to keep well to the left, at a right-hand bend. Which of the following best explains the reason for the advice?

a) To enable you to see any hazard sooner

b) To allow super-elevation of the road have effect

c) To avoid skidding of the road

d) To allow for overtaking by faster- moving vehicle

12) **Hot weather affects a part of your vehicle. Which of the following part of your vehicle will be most affected during hot weather?**

a) Tyres

b) Brake

c) Steering

d) Engine

13) **When applying a brake, which of the following road conditions need extra care?**

a) Sunny condition

b) Wet condition

c) Icy and snowy condition

d) Loose condition

14) **Skidding often occurs while turning on a wet surface. Knowing what to do, help you from driving off- road or tumbling to the side. What is the best action to take when you observe that your vehicle is skidding to the left while turning to the right?**

a) Carefully engage the neutral gear

b) Carefully apply your brake

c) Carefully steer to the left while braking

d)   Carefully steer to the right

15) **Skids don't just happen, and certain factors caused them. All the factors listed except one does not lead to skid?**

a)   The driver

b)   The steering

c)   The road condition

d)   The vehicle

16) **What does Contraflow mean?**

a)   An arrangement that allows a vehicle to drive in its usual direction

b)   A temporary arrangement that transfers vehicles moving in the same direction to share half of the lane

c)   Permanent closure of the road for other traffic function while making use of one lane

d)   A temporary arrangement where traffic is transferred to use the lane of the vehicle moving in the opposite direction

17) **Construction work is ongoing in your traffic direction, and you are to share the same lane with vehicles coming in the opposite direction. Which of the following is recommended while merging into the contraflow?**

a)   Enter the lane at a low speed and at the right time

b) Enter the lane at a faster speed to avoid traffic build-up

c) Follow other vehicles closely to avoid traffic build-up

d) Contraflow can be dangerous to drive through

18) **When you observe that you are being followed too closely by a vehicle, what should you do?**

a) Speed up to give a sufficient gap between you and the following vehicle behind.

b) Slow down to increase the distance between you and the vehicle in front.

c) Speed up and put your hazard light on to indicate the hazard caused by the following vehicle.

d) Drift a bit to the shoulder to give room for the vehicle to overtake.

19) **Strong winds affect two-wheeled vehicles easily. When overtaking such vehicles, what should you do?**

a) Always pass as quickly as possible.

b) Sound your horn any time you need to overtake.

c) Slow down while overtaking.

d) Give ample space in-between.

20) It is not advisable to do the following while driving when it is foggy, wet, and visibility is greatly reduced?

a) Use your front and rear fog lights.

b) Follow up closely with the front vehicle.

c) Maintain a slow speed.

d) Allow doubling the normal stopping distance.

21) You found yourself on an icy road, and the vehicle seems a bit unstable. What should you do to avoid loss of control?

a) Keep low speed while using the highest gear possible.

b) Use the hand brake intermittently

c) Carefully apply your brake and repeatedly

d) Avoid skidding and accelerating further

22) You are travelling at 60 mph on a Sunday afternoon; suddenly, you saw a bend twenty metres ahead. Such late vision is a result of:

a) The road marking must have been faded.

b) Lack of concentration

c) Short-sightedness

d) Lack of necessary road signs

23) A friend requested for your advice about his journey. He has been invited for an event in

another city that would take him almost forty-five minutes of drive in good weather conditions. It has been snowing for a few days, and ice can be seen on the road. What advice can you give to him?

a)   Remove the necessary ice on your vehicle that will affect your vision and hit the road.

b)   Make sure to go with your map and follow up with the weather report.

c)   Don't travel.

d)   Get rid of the ice on the road.

24) **Which of the following should you do to reduce wheel spin while travelling on an icy surface?**

a)   Accelerate quickly and brake gently

b)   Brake quickly when required

c)   Steering quickly away from possible skidding

d)   Brake and accelerate gently

25) **When driving down a steep hill, the vehicle always speeds up. This makes it difficult while trying to stop. Therefore you are advised to use a low gear while driving and apply the brake gently. How convincing is this advice?**

a)   Very convincing

b)   Not convincing

c)   Partially convincing

d)   Indifferent

26) When a driver goes over the speed hump without reducing its speed, what effect could this have on the car?

a) Damage the gearbox
b) Damage engine
c) Damage steering and suspension
d) Damage brake system

27) It has been raining, and the road surface is wet and your tyre has poor contact with the road surface. What could be the effect of these conditions on your driving?

a) The stopping distance of the vehicle will be maintained due to the contact points on the tyres
b) The car will properly stop when the brake is applied due to the contact of the tyres and the road surface
c) The stopping distance will increase due to less contact point on the tyres
d) The braking system will fail due to poor contact point on the tyres

28) The anti-lock brake should not be deployed in which of the following situation?

a) When braking normally

b) When braking harshly

c) When braking aggressively

d) When braking for a sudden stop

29) In which of the following road surface conditions will anti-lock become not effective?

a) Tarred road

b) Gravel road

c) Concrete road

d) Asphalt road

30) The anti-lock system will be more effective in which of the following situation?

a) While braking to enter an intersection

b) While braking to allow for pedestrian crossing

c) While braking to make a U-turn

d) While braking to avoid an accident

31) You intend to park your vehicle along the road on a sloppy downward road. Which direction should you face your front tyres?

a) Turn towards the road

b) Straight facing the road

c) Turn toward the side kerb

d) Turn at a right angle to the car

32) **What is the advantage of driving a four-wheel vehicle?**

a) In improves fuel economy

b) There is extra grip on the road

c) There is enough room for passengers

d) The engine capacity enhances the functionality of the vehicle.

33) **Your tyres have made a depression in the snow while trying to drive out. How can you drive the vehicle out without digging further?**

a) Use a high gear and slowly maneuver the vehicle forward and backward.

b) Use a low gear and drive the vehicle forward.

c) Use a low gear and slowly maneuver the vehicle forward and backward.

d) Use a high gear and drive the vehicle forward.

34) **The anti-lock brake system helps you to achieve one of the following?**

a) To brake effectively in a gravel environment

b) To brake firmly in an icy condition

c) Brake and steer at the same time

d) Effectively brake and steer in poor weather conditions

35) **Driving in an anti-lock brake car can be helpful to prevent the brake from locking. Which of the**

following condition is the anti-lock system most effective?

a) Wet condition

b) Snow condition

c) Loose road surface

d) Dry asphalt surface

36) **The anti-lock brake is useful to stop the wheel from locking. When does the anti-lock brake get activated?**

a) When driving at a high speed

b) When driving at a low speed

c) When braking gently at an emergency

d) When braking firmly at an emergency

37) **You have an emergency: thus, the need to travel is important. You have to drive through an icy road to your destination. What must you do?**

a) Always make sure to brake firmly to avoid an accident.

b) Drive at a low gear through the icy road.

c) Be ready to steer as you go as you go along for effective response swiftly.

d) Make sure that the anti-lock brake is effective.

38) **Driving downhill requires extra care and attention. How can you most operate your vehicle engine to support the stopping of the vehicle?**

a) Be ready to select the reverse gear.

b) Use high gear at low rev.

c) Change progressively to a lower gear.

d) Clutch down or engage the neutral and keep the steering firm.

39) Your anti-lock brake functions effectively but you release the brake before the car almost came to a stop. How does this action affect your brake?

a) The car slowly comes to a stop.

b) The car stopped as soon as the pedal is released.

c) The anti-lock brake will be disabled.

d) The car anti-brake engages the wheel to stop

40) The following road conditions are the two-second time gap used to determine the gap between vehicles?

a) Dry road condition

b) Wet road condition

c) Snowy condition

d) Icy condition

41) Which of the following do you normally observe when you drive along an icy road?

a) The tyres make almost no noise.

b) There is a whistling sound when driving at high speed.

c) There is always a screeching sound.

d) The steering becomes a bit stiff to turn.

42) It rained two days earlier before embarking on your journey. The weather is currently dry, but you just passed through a high pool of water. What should you do before you build up speed again?

a) Check the effectiveness of your steering.

b) Check that your brake is working properly.

c) Check that the tyres and wheel are still in good condition.

d) Ensure that the speedometer indicator in functional.

43) **You are driving on a Saturday afternoon under a good weather condition while suddenly a child came running across the road. What must you do in this emergency?**

a) Turn the steering away from the child.

b) Apply your brake firmly and quickly.

c) Immediately apply your brake with caution.

d) Slow down with caution.

44) Coasting means driving with the clutch held down or the gear lever in neutral. Which of the following is false?

a) It allows the vehicle to freewheel.

b) It reduces the driver's control of the vehicle.

c) It enables the engine to drive the wheels as you pull through a corner.

d) It offers assistance to the engine braking as you slow the car.

Answer To Questions on Safety Margins

No	1	2	3	4	5	6	7	8	9
Answers	C	C	D	C	B	B	D	D	D

No	10	11	12	13	14	15	16	17	18
Answers	A	A	A	C	D	B	D	A	B

No	19	20	21	22	23	24	25	26	27
Answers	D	B	A	B	C	D	A	C	C

No	28	29	30	31	32	33	34	35	36
Answers	A	B	D	C	B	A	C	D	B

No	37	38	39	40	41	42	43	44	
Answers	B	C	C	A	A	B	B	C	

Chapter 5

Hazard Awareness

1) **Bridges are built to have more headroom at the centre. Thus, when driving under a bridge, which vehicle do you expect to see driving in the middle of the road?**

    a) Minibus

    b) Car

    c) Lorry

    d) Tricycle

2) **What should you do while turning right at a junction?**

    a) Follow the road markings.

    b) Follow closely with the vehicle ahead of you.

    c) Drive slowly until you can see both sides of the road.

    d) Drive a bit to the centre of the road to have more turning radius.

3) **What action should you take as you approach a bend before making a turn?**

    a) Drive a bit faster for effective maneuvering.

    b) Adjust your speed and select the correct gear.

    c) Drive to the middle of the road.

    d) Turn on your hazard light.

4) **When you brake late and harshly as you change direction, what effect will it have on your vehicle?**

   a) The grip of the vehicle on the road is reduced.

   b) The vehicle comes to a sudden stop.

   c) Skidding is avoided as long as you steer carefully in the right direction.

   d) The anti-lock brake will be disengaged

5) **When you come across this sign at a certain point of the road, what does it mean**

   a) Go straight ahead

   b) Left turning arrow ahead

   c) Sharp deviation of a route to the left

   d) Caution bend ahead

6) **If you come across the sign below as you drive through the town, what should you do?**

   a) Drive quickly to pass before pedestrian arrives

b) Sound your horn to alert pedestrians of your presence.

c) Flag down the vehicle behind you as you attempt to stop.

d) Slow down and be ready to stop

7) One of the following options is the best way to prevent hazards while driving?

a) Drive with the hazard light on

b) Be ready to sound your horn as soon as you observe a hazard

c) Look well ahead to prepare for any hazard

d) Always make sure you tailgate the vehicle in front of you

8) The sign below can be found on which kind of vehicle?

a) Cars more than 3m long

b) Cars less than 3m long

c) Vehicles more than 13m long

d) Buses

9) You are driving along a narrow road with cars parked along both sides of the road. You must be on the lookout for hazards. Which of the

following three hazards are most likely to occur in such a situation?

a) Car driving along the road

b) A pedestrian trying to cross the road between cars

c) Cars attempting to leave the parking lot

d) The parked car door opened suddenly

10) What should you do when you arrived at a junction with the stop sign, as shown in the picture?

a) You must stop if you are turning to the right

b) You must stop before the line and assess the situation

c) Observe the situation from far and proceed or stop if necessary

d) Slow down just before the line and cross gently

11) **As you approached a junction and observed that the traffic lights have failed, what should you do?**

   a)   Proceed without stopping

   b)   Stop to allow for any vehicle crossing

   c)   Proceed with caution and be ready to stop

   d)   Avoid using the route of a malfunctioning traffic light

12) **When you come across the sign below, what should you do?**

   a)   Slow down and be on the lookout for children crossing.

   b)   Be proactive and assess the road from far and then drive on if it is clear.

   c)   Continue driving but keep your hazard light on

   d)   Sound your horn and flash your headlight as you drive

13) **You were driving on a major road and slowed down as you come close to the T-Junction. A car**

suddenly pulls out of a corner street. What should you do?

a) Call the traffic control and inform them of the incident.

b) Calm down and let the driver proceed.

c) Sound your horn and overtake the car as soon as possible.

d) Flash your headlight and shout out to the driver.

14) **You are at a junction with the traffic light turned red when a cyclist pulls up just ahead of you. If you are to turn left at the junction, what should you do?**

a) Make a turn before the cyclist makes a turn.

b) Exercise patience for the cyclist to pass

c) Sound your horn for the cyclist to know you are behind.

d) Flag the cyclist down as you turn left.

15) **Concentration is very important when embarking on a long journey; it is recommended that a break be taken. How long should the break take?**

a) 10 minutes after every one hour

b) 10 minutes after every two hour

c) 15 minutes after every one hour

d) 15 minutes after every two hour

16) **What should you do before you overtake a long vehicle?**

   a) Pull back to have a clear view of the road ahead.

   b) Change to a lower gear and accelerate past the long vehicle.

   c) Change to a higher gear and quickly overtake.

   d) Flash your headlight indicating to the long vehicle driver that you a passing.

17) **For which of the following reason should you be tolerant of elderly drivers on the road while driving?**

   a) They could react slowly to hazards.

   b) They might not be able to read the traffic sign.

   c) They may have expired documents for driving.

   d) To see the traffic lights and signs might be difficult for them.

Start next

18) **While driving along a road with double side parking, how much room should you give to the parked cars?**

   a) Same with of the size of the car

   b) Drive in the centre of the road

   c) Drive about one metre or the width of an opened door

d) Leave available the width capable of allowing a pedestrian to pass along

19) What should you do when you drove to the point of school traffic control?

a) Slow down and drive carefully

b) Slow down and stop by the school traffic sign

c) Be careful and proceed with care when the school traffic controller displays the sign

d) Stop and wait for further instruction from the school traffic controller

20) What does this traffic sign represent?

a) Slippery road

b) Skid sign

c) Oil in the road

d) Double bend

21) You are driving along a double carriageway when you saw a pelican crossing. The pedestrians are crossing from the other side of the road and not yet at the island. What should you do?

a) Proceed since the pedestrians have not yet reached the island.

b) Stop and wait for the pedestrians to cross both carriageways.

c) Alert the pedestrian of your presence by sounding your horn.

d) Slow down and proceed carefully.

22) You are driving along a less busy road at 60 mph; you suddenly saw a small animal on the road. What should you do?

a) Avoid killing the animal by swerving away

b) Immediately apply the emergency brake

c) Proceed with your journey safely.

d) Sound your horn and flash your headlight to scare the animal aware.

23) You have just crossed the white line at a level crossing before the amber light comes on. What should you do?

a) Pull back and maintain a position before the white line.

b) Proceed with your driving.

c) Just switch on your hazard light.

d) Stop immediately after the half-barrier.

24) **You are late for an important meeting when you came to a zebra crossing. You stopped for pedestrians to cross, but unfortunately, there are three elderly ones among them. They seem to be taken much time to cross. What should you do?**

a) Wait for the pedestrians to finish crossing.

b) Alert the pedestrians that cars are waiting by sounding your horn.

c) Cross immediately behind the last pedestrian.

d) Wave on the pedestrians to cross faster.

25) **What should you do when you find yourself close to a slow-moving vehicle approaching a junction?**

a) Reduce your speed and create a chance for overtaking.

b) Proceed without stopping.

c) Take the necessary safety precaution and overtake.

d) Follow behind the vehicle until you pass the junction.

26) **Negative attitudes and reckless driving are common on the road. How should you handle a driver's negative attitude while driving, especially when you are tired?**

a) Flash your headlight repeatedly.

b) Stop and take a break.

c) Sound your horn to the hearing of the driver.

d) Shout loud at the driver.

27) What is the need for calming traffic measures on the road?

a) Safeguard the vehicle

b) Reduce accident impact on the driver

c) Reduce accident impact on the passengers

d) Protect pedestrians

28) Towns and City's names are written on the road surface or hang under the soffit of a bridge for one of the following reasons?

a) To indicate the next location.

b) To stop the indiscriminate swerving of vehicles.

c) To alert you of location with hazard situation.

d) To alert you to change lane on time.

29) What does the sign below represent?

a) Double lane

b) Double carriageway

c) No overtaking

d) Yield to the vehicle on the right

30) What does the sign below represent?

a) Uneven road surface

b) Bridge over the road

c) A ford vehicle company yard next

d) Water across the road

31) The solid white line along the road means?

a) Edge of the carriageway

b) Continuous road ahead

c) Single lane road

d) It represents the center of the road

32) What should you do when you approach a level crossing with a twin flashing red lights on?

a) Prepare to stop

b) Stop

c) Proceed

d) Nothing

33) **Before overtaking a leading vehicle, which of the following is not a correction?**

a) Make sure there is no oncoming vehicle.

b) Make sure that the road width is wide enough for your action.

c) Make sure that the leading has a higher speed than yours.

d) Make sure that there is no junction ahead.

34) **After being in a queue for some minutes, what should you do before driving off?**

a) Check nearside for cyclists.

b) Drive off immediately.

c) Confirm the clearance with the vehicle behind you.

d) Alert nearby vehicle by sounding the horn.

35) **Where can you find this sign?**

a) Before a zebra crossing

b) Before a junction

c) Before a pelican crossing

d) Before pulling off a major road

36) **You are driving along a four-lane road. You observe an overhead sign with one Red Cross sign and three-speed signs. If you are driving on the lane with the Red Cross sign, what should you do next?**

a) Proceed with the journey.

b) Safely reduce the speed of the vehicle.

c) Carefully increase the speed of the vehicle.

d) Safely leave the lane.

37) **When does this sign mean?**

a) Articulated vehicle ahead.

b) Right turn ahead

c) Turning ahead

d) Caution

38) **You want to enter a particular road in an unfamiliar area. And you see this line, What does it mean?**

a) Cars allow

b) Motorcycle allow

c) No motor vehicle allow

d) Road closed

39) **Hazard warning lights can be effective in which of the following cases.**

a) While making a U-Turn

b) When there is an obstruction

c) While entering a major road

d) When signaling improper driving to a road user

Answers To Questions on Hazards Awareness

No	1	2	3	4	5	6	7	8	9
Answers	C	C	B	A	C	D	C	C	A,C &D

No	10	11	12	13	14	15	16	17	18
Answers	B	C	A	B	B	D	A	A	C

No	19	20	21	22	23	24	25	26	27
Answers	D	A	A	C	B	A	D	B	D

No	28	29	30	31	32	33	34	35	36
Answers	A	C	B	A	B	C	A	B	D

No	37	38	39
Answers	B	C	B

Chapter 6

General Questions

1) **One out of these categories of road user is not vulnerable road user**

   a) Cyclist

   b) Truck

   c) Pedestrians

   d) Horse riders

2) **What does this sign mean?**

   a) Pedestrian crossing

   b) Cyclist crossing

   c) Shared footpath

   d) No access for pedestrian and cyclist

3) **You are making a left turn to a minor road. Pedestrians were already on the road crossing. What should you do?**

   a) Stop and wait for the pedestrian to finish crossing.

   b) Proceed slowly while the pedestrians cross.

   c) Follow up immediately behind the pedestrian.

d) Sound your horn and signal to the pedestrian to move up.

4) **You want to turn into a side road, and you want to avoid any road user to hit your vehicle from the side. What should you do?**

a) Signal to the correct side and sound your horn.

b) Look over your shoulder to make sure that the road is clear.

c) Indicate your direction and drive on.

d) Follow the vehicle in front of you closely to stop another vehicle from taking the space.

5) **You are driving to a police station, and there are no school children in sight. You saw a school crossing patrol with this sign. What should you do?**

a) Proceed with your journey

b) Slow down and stop

c) Slow down and proceed at a reduced speed

d) Ignore the school crossing patrol because no one is crossing

6) You are driving on the road and saw a pedestrian carrying a white stick with a red reflective band standing by the road's side. Who could such man be?

a) A cripple

b) A deaf

c) A deaf and blind

d) A homeless

7) What should you do when you drive near to pedestrian with a white cane?

a) Proceed as normal

b) Flash your headlight

c) Slow down and prepare to stop

d) Sound your horn as you cross

8) Which of the following needs an extra room while overtaken?

a) Tow vehicles

80

b) Mixer trucks

c) Double axel vehicles

d) Motorcycles

9) **You are behind a motorcyclist that is travelling slowly; how should you approach him?**

a) Sound your horn to alert him you are behind.

b) Move closer to him and rev your vehicle while clutching down.

c) Overtaken him as quickly as possible.

d) Follow behind patiently and observe his action.

10) **How should a motorcyclist dress while riding at night?**

a) Wear a hand glove and long trousers

b) Put a comfortable shoes for riding

c) Wear a helmet

d) Wear reflective clothing or strip

11) **You are at a junction and are about to join the major. Which of the following road users should you keep on the lookout for?**

a) Taxi drivers

b) Cyclist

c) Truck driver

d) Bus driver

12) **Inexperience is a stage in driving that is commonly seen on the road. When you observe that an inexperienced driver is driving in front of you, how do you handle the situation?**

   a) Avoid him by overtaken as fast as possible.

   b) Flash your headlight continuously until you are observed.

   c) Follow patiently and wait for their reaction.

   d) Sound your horn to indicate your presence.

13) **Which of the following light should you use when driving on a motorway at night?**

   a) Dipped headlight

   b) Hazard light

   c) Hazard and dipped headlight

   d) Break light

14) **Which of the following action should you take if your vehicle breaks down on a motorway?**

   a) Stop on the point of breakdown and call for help immediately.

   b) Park on the hard shoulder with your light on.

   c) Park on the speed lane with the hazard light on.

   d) Place your caution sign on the road to alert oncoming vehicles.

15) As you drive along a motorway at night, you discover that you are moving too close to the amber reflective light. Which part of the road are you?

a) Close to the hard shoulder.

b) Between the carriageway and the central reserve.

c) Between two lanes in the same carriageway.

d) Between the hard shoulder and the speed lane.

16) You are driving on a motorway; you saw a mandatory speed limit placed above the hard shoulder. What does this mean?

a) Do not drive on the hard shoulder

b) No parking on the hard shoulder

c) Temporary parking allowed on the hard shoulder.

d) Using the hard shoulder should be allowed.

17) While driving on the road. what speed limit will you maintain on the road with street lighting?

a) 30 mph

b) 40 mph

c) 35 mph

d) 45 mph

18) A vehicle is seen towing a small caravan on a motorway, what will be the maximum speed limit?

a) 70 mph

b) 60 mph

c) 50 mph

d) 40 mph

19) Where are you likely to find the road marking below?

a) Before a bend

b) Close to a pedestrian crossing

c) At a motorway slip road

d) At a motorway bypass

20) What does this sign mean?

a) Hump bridge

b) Calming hump

c) Bridge

d) Arch bridge

21) You are approaching an exit road when you saw a pedestrian just beginning to cross the road; you should

a) Proceed with your driving as you have the right of way

b) Yield to the pedestrian to finish crossing

c) Sound your horn and proceed

d) Signal to the pedestrian to proceed with the crossing

22) On which part of the road should you be driving on a double carriageway with three lanes provided the road ahead is clear?

a) The left side of the lane

b) Middle of the lane

c) The right side of the lane

d) Along the hard shoulder

Answers To General Questions

No	1	2	3	4	5	6	7	8	9
Answers	B	C	A	B	B	C	C	D	D

No	10	11	12	13	14	15	16	17	18
Answers	D	B	C	A	B	B	D	A	B

No	19	20	21	22
Answers	C	A	B	A

Chapter 7

Tips for Passing the DVSA Test

This book has all the theoretical lessons you need to nail your practical driving test. You need not worry much if you have studied hard using this useful material, knowing that everything question is a potential tip for passing your theory and practical test.

The first information you need to have is that there is no need for anxiety for the practical test. This is because your driving instructor will have to put you through the entire rudiment needed to pass the practical on the first trial.

If you are ready for the test, make sure the following tips are adhered to:

1. **Do your driving training.**

   Registration with a registered driving school is the first step to your quest to have your driving license on your hand. There are various driving instructors out there, but you can do your research or inquire from those you know have done the test earlier on their thought of an instructor that can give you the training and knowledge you need to know how to drive and pass the test. As part of your inquiry, make sure that the school has a good traffic sign available and positioned for your practice classes.

2. **Practice**

   Look for a good instructor and sign up; know your purpose of engaging an instructor and paying for his services. If this sacrifice is worth it, then you need to make an effort to learn. As you learn, practice what you have learned. Continuous practice is the only way to perfect your driving skill and become a pro. It also boosts your confidence.

   Don't be in a hurry to schedule a driving test without perfecting your move; else, you will not get a good mark and will be forced to repeat the test - this could be very frustrating.

   Allow your driving instructor to access and advice you when to go for a test or another lesson. Instructors are always good at the game.

3. **Know your route**

   There are common routes that are normally used for the driving test. Get familiar with the route together with the road signs and plan your practice to suit the routes.

4. **Do not be anxious**

   Don't ever be afraid of anything; otherwise, you will be prone to mistakes, and you find yourself shaking. Anxiety is for those that are not prepared. If you are ready with the tip given here, then you need not be anxious. Wait a minute; some people are generally anxious when they have to do something new. Ok, if this is your case, then you need to find a way to kill the anxiety. One thing I recommend is to have a short ride in the morning before going for the test. This will help put you in the mood and put your anxiety level down. Just tell yourself, 'I did this morning. It's the same thing'. Take a deep breath to calm yourself.

5. **A Mistake is not a failure.**

Do not allow your first mistake to bother you, brace up, and proceed normally but very observant. Always look out for the road signs, observe your mirrors, and watch out for other road users. Minor faults will not fail you, but the major fault will.

6. **The eyesight check**

Do you have a sight issue? This information has to be provided to the examiners beforehand because you are expected to tell the plate number of a car about twenty metres ahead of you. You can exaggerate to about twenty-two metres to be on the safe side.

7. **Show me, tell me**

You will be expected to answer a question from the test instructor, which will involve your driving and vehicle knowledge. This book helps you answer such questions easily.

Printed in Great Britain
by Amazon